Slim Goodbody's Inside Guide to Pets

CATS

By Slim Goodbody

Illustrations: Ben McGinnis

Consultant: James Montgomery,
Doctor of Veterinary Medicine and
Kate Bergen Pierce, Doctor of Veterinary Medicine

Gareth Stevens
Publishing

Dedication: For our cats Le Pigeon and Caesar and especially for Luke, the boy who loves them.

Please visit our web site at: www.garethstevens.com
For a free color catalog describing Gareth Stevens Publishing's list
of high-quality books, call 1-800-542-2595 (USA) or 1-800-387-3178 (Canada).
Gareth Stevens Publishing's fax: 1-877-542-2596

Library of Congress Cataloging-in-Publication Data

Burstein, John.
  Cats / John Burstein.
    p. cm. — (Slim Goodbody's inside guide to pets)
  Includes bibliographical references and index.
    ISBN-10: 0-8368-8954-1 ISBN-13: 978-0-8368-8954-3 (lib. bdg.)
    1. Cats—Juvenile literature. I. Title.
  SF445.7.B86 2008
  636.8—dc22   2007033452

This edition first published in 2008 by
Gareth Stevens Publishing
A Weekly Reader® Company
1 Reader's Digest Road
Pleasantville, NY 10570-7000 USA

Copyright © 2008 by Gareth Stevens, Inc.
Text and artwork copyright © 2008 by Slim Goodbody Corp. (www.slimgoodbody.com).
Slim Goodbody is a registered trademark of Slim Goodbody Corp.

Photos: (t = top, b = bottom, r = right, c = center, m = middle)
© iStock International Inc. p. 1, p. 5t, 5b, p. 6br, p. 7t, 7b, p. 8b, p. 9t, 9b,
p. 10, p. 12t, 12b, p. 13(all), p. 15m, 15b, p.17t, 17b, p. 18t, p. 19t, 19b,
p. 20b, p. 21t, 21b, p. 22b, p. 23t, 23b, p. 24b, p. 25t, p. 26b, p. 27t, 27b,
p. 28m, 28m, 28b p. 29t, 29b; © www.skullsunlimited.com p. 6t;
© clipart.com p. 6br; © Tammy West p. 3, p. 4, 29b, © CORBIS p. 17.
Illustrations: Ben McGinnis, Adventure Advertising

Managing Editor: Valerie J. Weber, Wordsmith Ink
Designer: Tammy West, Westgraphix LLC
Gareth Stevens Senior Managing Editor: Lisa M. Guidone
Gareth Stevens Creative Director: Lisa Donovan

Printed in the United States of America

1 2 3 4 5 6 7 8 9 10 10 09 08

CONTENTS

Words that appear in the glossary are printed in **boldface** type the first time they occur in the text.

MEET THE QUEEN OF CATS

Hello! My name is Cleopatra. My friends call me Cleo. I was named after Cleopatra, the **ancient** queen of Egypt. History says she was very beautiful. My owners gave me this name because they think I am beautiful too. My owners say I am the most beautiful animal in the world. I do not agree. I think mice look far more beautiful . . . especially when I am hungry. **YUM!**

A Tail from Long Ago

I have lots of interesting things to tell you. For example, did you know that cats and people have lived together for over five thousand years? The ancient Egyptians used cats to stop rats and mice from stealing grain.

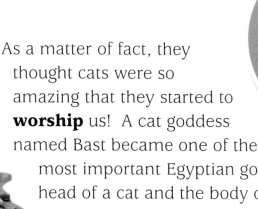

As a matter of fact, they thought cats were so amazing that they started to **worship** us! A cat goddess named Bast became one of the most important Egyptian gods. Bast had the head of a cat and the body of a woman. She was worshipped for over two thousand years! Cats worked all over the ancient world. The Greeks kept cats to hunt rats and mice. The Vikings used us as rat catchers on their ships. Frederick the Great, king of Prussia, thought so highly of cats that he made them the official guards of his army's supplies.

As you can see, cats have been popular for a long time. Today, there are more than 90 million pet cats in the United States alone. By the way, most of my human friends like to pat me. If you are interested, I might find some time for a belly rub.

Cleo's Clues

If you are bringing home a new cat, please give her time to explore and get used to her **surroundings**. It will take time for your new family member to get comfortable, especially if there are other pets around.

My skeleton gives my body its shape.

It holds me up and protects the soft parts inside me.

Cats have more bones than people do. People's skeletons are made up of 206 bones. We have about 244 bones. I say "about 244" because some cats have as many as 250 bones, and some cats have only 230.

The exact number depends on our toes and tails. Most cats have five toes on each front paw and four toes on each back paw. Some cats, however, are born with one or two extra toes on each foot. Cats with more toes have more bones.

When it comes to tails, a cat with a long tail has more bones than a cat with a short tail. There are even some cats with no tails, such as the Manx.

FUN FACT

Our tails help us balance when we climb trees, walk along chair backs, or tiptoe across high shelves. If we run and change direction quickly, our tails help keep us from skidding and falling.

I'm in Great Shape

I have five more bones in my spine than you do. These extra bones allow me to twist and bend. I can lie down and roll up into an O shape. I can also stand up and curve my back into a U shape with my belly almost touching the floor. When I want to clean myself, I can turn my body so my tongue can reach the fur on the center of my back.

Cleo's Clues

When cats jump or fall from high places, they can get hurt. If you live in a high building, make sure to keep your window screens shut. Even if you live on the first floor, your cat can jump off the railing or wriggle through the bars and escape outdoors.

I can also squeeze through openings the width of my head! How? I can squish my shoulder and chest bones together tightly because my tiny collarbones are not attached to my shoulders. Your big collarbones are connected to your shoulder bones. You could never slip through an opening the size of your head.

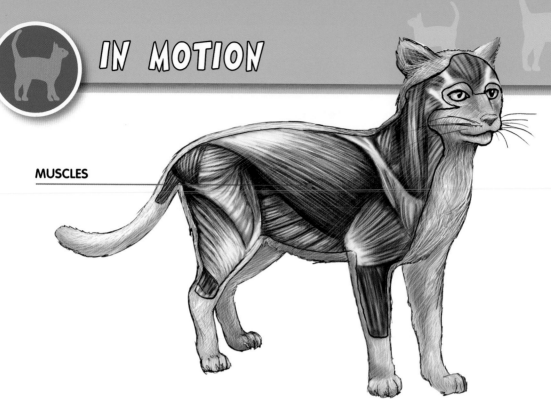

MUSCLES

I have about 517 muscles in my body. You have about 650 muscles. Even though you have more muscles, I can do things you would find amazing. For example, I can jump nine times my own height. To understand how **incredible** this is, imagine a 5-foot (1.5-meter) tall human jumping nine times his own height. If he could match my jumping ability, he would be able to leap 45 feet (14 m) in the air!

I can leap this high because my leg muscles are powerful. They can push off from the ground like a rocket ship blasting off. My leg muscles are also **flexible**. I can stretch my front legs wide apart to wrap them around a toy and hold it close. I can tuck my front paws under my chest when I crouch down. I can curve my legs behind my head when I wash behind my ears. I can even turn my paws over to wash under and between my claws.

Faster Than a Speeding Human

I am a fast runner. I can run about 30 miles (48 kilometers) an hour. The fastest human can only run about 23 miles (37 km) an hour.

I'm speedy because of the muscles in my spine. I have muscles between each **vertebra** in my spine. These muscles let me stretch out really far. As I run, I leap and stretch out. Each leap carries me forward three times the length of my entire body!

Cleo's Clues

Playing with your cat is a fun way to keep her active. Throw a stuffed mouse across the room for her to pounce on. Put **catnip** in a toy and let her chase it. Encourage her to follow you around the house. Every little bit of exercise helps. Try for twenty minutes of play or exercise every day.

Over their lifetimes, cats and humans both grow two sets of teeth. Cats get twenty-six baby teeth and thirty adult teeth. Humans get twenty baby teeth and thirty-two grown-up teeth.

My teeth grow in a lot faster than yours do. My baby teeth started coming in when I was only four weeks old. Human babies' teeth don't start to come in until the children are about six months old.

Born To Be Wild

Before I tell you any more, remember one thing. Today, most of my food comes in cans and bags, but I was really born to hunt. There will always be a bit of wildcat in my blood. My teeth were designed to kill animals and tear meat from their bones.

My canine teeth are my strongest and sharpest teeth. They stab, hold, and tear the meat from the animals I kill.

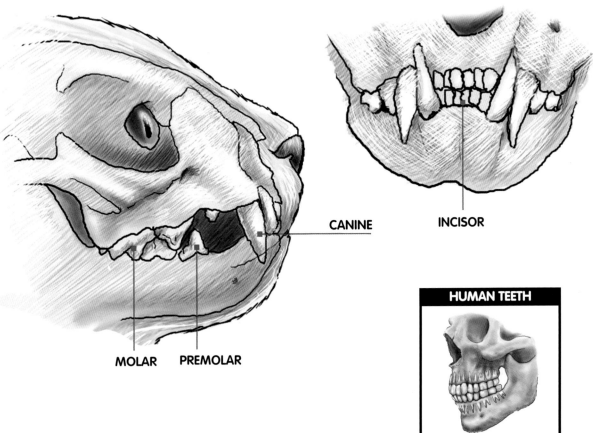

CANINE

INCISOR

MOLAR   PREMOLAR

My smaller incisors help me rip and pull off feathers and fur. They also help me pull meat away from the bones. My premolars and molars cut the meat down into chunks that are small enough to swallow.

One Big Gulp

It may sound a bit strange, but I cannot chew my food like you do. One reason is because of the shape of my molars. You have flat molars. Flat molars let you grind and chew. I have pointy molars. Pointy molars let me cut food up but not chew it. I swallow most of my food whole.

Cleo's Clues
You may need to take your cat to a **vet** if he has very bad breath or red and swollen gums, paws at his mouth, or refuses to eat hard food. Your vet will probably suggest you brush your cat's teeth about once each week.

I love my claws. They are so useful. When I climb a tree, I dig my claws into the bark to hold on firmly. If I am on a slippery floor, my claws help keep me from slipping. If I am hunting, my claws help me catch mice, rats, and other animals. If I am in a fight, my claws help me defend myself.

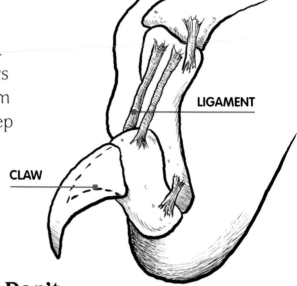

LIGAMENT

CLAW

Now You See Them, Now You Don't

I have four claws on each back paw and five claws on each front paw. When you look at my paws, you might not see my claws. I can pull them in when I do not need them. The scientific word describing claws that can be pulled in is *retractable*. I keep my claws pulled in most of the time because it helps keep them sharp. If my claws were out all the time, they would quickly get worn down on the hard ground. They would also get caught on rugs and carpets.

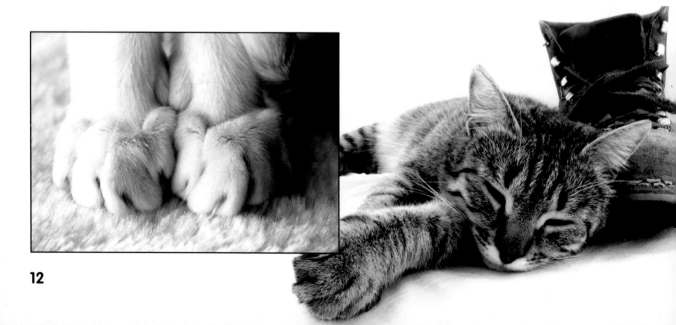

FUN FACT

All members of the cat family have retractable claws except one — the cheetah.

Keeping my claws in also helps me move silently when I am on the prowl and sneaking up on a bird or mouse. **Shhhhhh.**

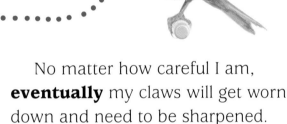

No matter how careful I am, **eventually** my claws will get worn down and need to be sharpened. To keep my claws in top form, I need to scratch things. Why? Well, my claw nails grow in layers. When I scratch, I get rid of the outer and duller layer of my nail. With this layer gone, a nice, sharp nail appears.

Cleo's Clues

Cats love to climb. We do it for safety reasons if we are being chased or just for fun and exercise. Please make sure we have somewhere safe to practice this skill. Otherwise, we might be tempted to streak up and down your curtains!

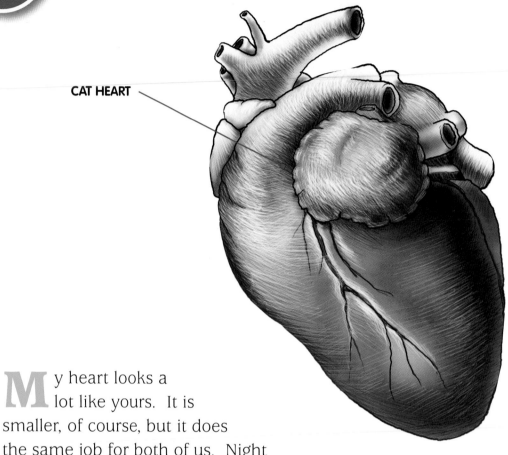

CAT HEART

My heart looks a lot like yours. It is smaller, of course, but it does the same job for both of us. Night and day, it pumps blood all through my body. The right side of my heart pumps blood to my lungs, and the left side pumps blood all through my body.

My heart beats about twice as fast as that of a grown-up human. Depending on what I'm doing, my heart beats between 150 and 240 beats a minute. (It beats faster when I run or I am excited.) A grown-up human's heart beats between 75 and 120 beats per minute.

Cleo's Clues

Being overweight is not good for your cat's heart. If you love your cat, please don't overfeed him. A fat cat is not a healthy cat.

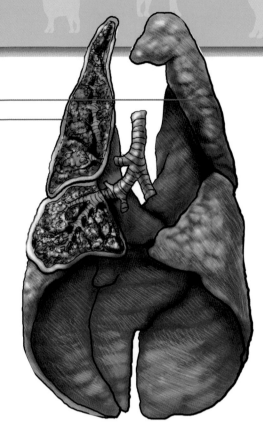

CAT LUNGS

Every Breath I Take

I also breathe faster than humans. I take about twenty to forty breaths a minute. I breathe faster when I'm chasing a mouse than when I am sleeping. A grown-up human breathes about twelve to twenty times per minute.

Panting, or breathing fast, helps me keep cool. You see, I do not sweat like you do. If I am hot, I cool down by breathing out warm air from my body and breathing in cooler air from outside. If I am panting a lot, however, it may be a sign that I am not feeling well and need to see the vet.

FUN FACT
Cats do not sweat through their skin like humans. However, they do sweat a little through their noses and the pads of their paws.

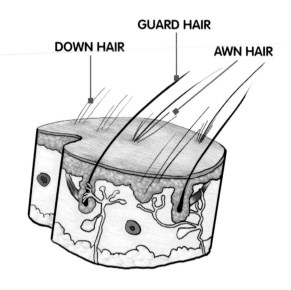

DOWN HAIR   **GUARD HAIR**   **AWN HAIR**

Cats love to dress up. That's why we always wear fur coats. I'm just kidding, of course. Actually, my fur coat protects my body. By the way, fur is just another name for hair. I have three kinds of hair on my body:

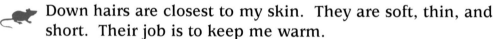

- Down hairs are closest to my skin. They are soft, thin, and short. Their job is to keep me warm.

- Awn hairs form my middle coat. They are tougher than the down hairs and have two main jobs. They help keep me warm, and they protect the down hairs.

- Guard hairs form my top coat. They are the longest, thickest, and straightest of my body's hairs. Their job is to protect the down and awn hairs from cold and keep water from soaking through to my skin.

My hair grows out from roots within my skin. Muscles lie next to these roots. When I am cold, these muscles cause my hairs to stick out straight, keeping me warm. If I am scared, these muscles also make my hairs stand out. Puffed up, I look bigger and scarier to an enemy.

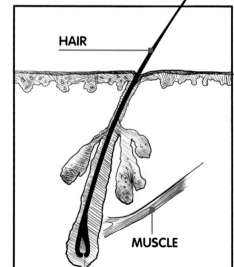

HAIR

MUSCLE

Coats of Many Colors

Cat coats come in all different lengths, colors, and patterns. Cat coats can be white, black, orange, gray, brown, cream, or silver. Cat coats can be up to three colors and striped or blotchy. Long ago, when cats lived in the wild, different patterns and colors help them blend in with their surroundings. By blending in, they could stay hidden when hunting or being hunted.

I have loose skin called a scruff at the back of my neck. A mother cat grips the scruff of her kittens to carry them. This loose skin lets us turn and face an enemy in a fight, even if that enemy has a grip on us.

Cleo's Clues

Your cat needs regular brushing. Brushing prevents her hair from getting stuck together and looking matted. Brushing also removes loose hair that she might lick and swallow. These loose hairs can form fur balls inside her belly that she will need to spit up.

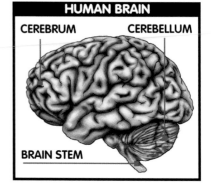

HUMAN BRAIN

CEREBRUM   CEREBELLUM

BRAIN STEM

My brain looks a lot like yours and has many of the same parts:

CEREBRUM: This is the part where I do my thinking.

CEREBELLUM: This is the part that controls my muscles.

BRAIN STEM: This is the part that connects my brain to my spine.

Cats are smart. Many people think we are the smartest pets of all. We have a really good memory. We can also solve problems, learn from our mistakes, and figure out how to get what we want. A cat friend of mine knows how to turn off the lights and use the toilet!

I learn new skills pretty much the way you do. I watch and imitate. I try something, and if it doesn't work the first time, I try again until it does work. For example, I learned to hunt by watching

my mother and practicing the moves she made. It took a while, but I finally learned just the right speed, height, and angle to leap and pounce on a bird or mouse.

Head over Paws

A cat's brain sends orders to its muscles very quickly. Imagine a cat falls from a height of 2 feet (61 centimeters). Imagine this cat starts its fall completely upside down with its feet pointed toward the sky. The brain sends orders so quickly that the cat can flip over and land on its feet. Within one-third of a second, it turns its head, twists its spine, lines up its legs, and arches its back to soften its landing.

Cleo's Clues

Cats are very curious. They will put just about anything into their mouths that seem interesting — including paper clips, pins, coins, and the small parts of kids' toys. If your cat grabs these things, she might choke, so be careful what you leave around. **19**

EYES SEE YOU

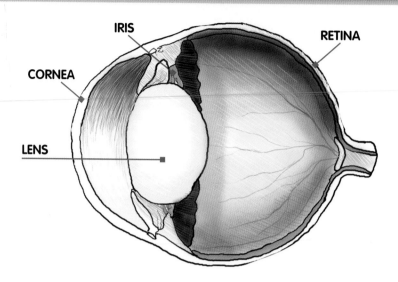

IRIS

RETINA

CORNEA

LENS

My beautiful big eyes face forward, just like yours. This position is unusual for a small animal. Most small animals have eyes on the sides of their heads. Animals with eyes that look out to the side are usually **prey** animals. They need a wide range of vision to see if any hunters are sneaking up on them. Cats are hunters, so my eyes face forward to see my prey in front of me.

Night Sight

You can see better in the daytime, but I can see six times better than you can in dim light. I cannot see in total darkness. If there is a little light, however, I can open my pupils really wide to let it in.

PUPIL

I also have a layer of cells the back of my eye. These cells catch and magnify dim light. If you shine a flashlight into my eyes in the dark, you'll see them shining. This layer of cells makes my eyes glow. If it's bright, I close my pupils down to narrow slits so I am not blinded by the light.

Kittens are all born with blue eyes. A few cats keep this color, but most gradually change eye color during the first few weeks of life.

Distance, Color, and Movement

You can see faraway things about four times better than I can. If you stand 80 feet (24.3 m) away from something and see it clearly, I need to stand 20 feet (6 m) away to see it just as well. My vision is sharpest 2 to 3 feet (61 to 91 cm) from my face.

I can see some colors but not as many as you can. Red, orange, yellow, and green all look like the same color to me. I also see both blue and violet as one color. I can recognize black and white, however.

I am really good at seeing something moving. When I hunt, I will pounce if a victim moves. I can miss the same animal if it is standing still.

Cleo's Clues

If you provide a nice comfortable safe spot for your cat to nap, he will really appreciate it. Cats spend about sixteen hours a day with their eyes closed.

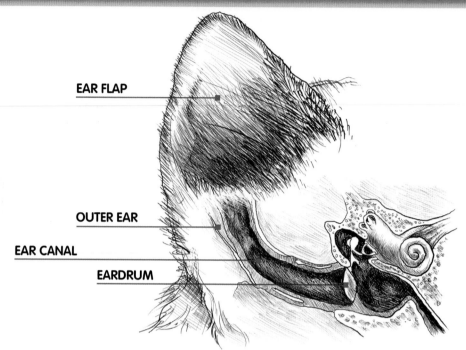

EAR FLAP

OUTER EAR

EAR CANAL

EARDRUM

When it comes to a sense of hearing, humans cannot even come close to matching my ability. There are several reasons for this:

Humans have six ear muscles. I have over thirty ear muscles. All these muscles let me turn and swivel my ears in many directions — forward, backward, and sideways. Not only that, I can move each ear separately! I can even move my body in one direction and point my ears in another direction. This ability comes in handy when I'm hunting and listening for my prey.

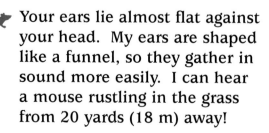

Your ears lie almost flat against your head. My ears are shaped like a funnel, so they gather in sound more easily. I can hear a mouse rustling in the grass from 20 yards (18 m) away!

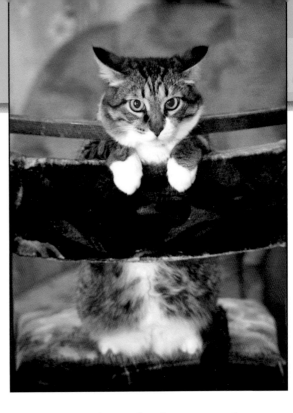

You may know that there are special dog whistles that make such a high sound that humans cannot hear it. Well, I can. As a matter of fact, I can even hear higher sounds than dogs can. In other words, you could blow a special cat whistle that I could hear and a dog could not.

Of course, if you blow that whistle, please don't expect me to come. I love my human family, but I do not like to follow orders very much.

Cleo's Clues

You can read your cat's mood by watching her ears. When she is content, her ears stand upright. When she is happy or excited, her ears will point forward. When she is angry or annoyed, her ears flatten and lie back. It is not a good idea to bother her when she is angry. She might scratch you by "accident."

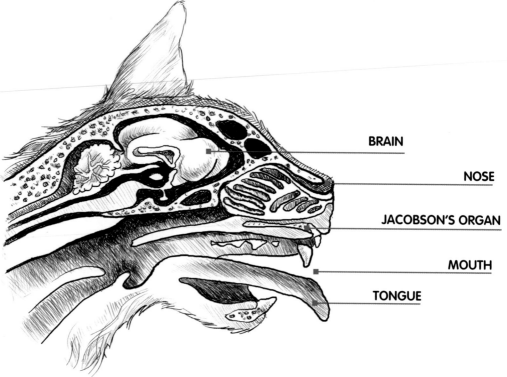

BRAIN

NOSE

JACOBSON'S ORGAN

MOUTH

TONGUE

I have a fantastic sense of smell, about fourteen times better than yours. I can smell about 200 million different odors. You do not even know that many of these odors exist.

My nose helps me hunt and avoid danger. I can often smell enemies long before I see them. I can also smell meals before they arrive in front of me.

My nose pad probably feels a bit like leather to you. It protects the softer parts of my nose. Nose pads can be black, reddish, or

pink. They are usually cool and a bit wet. Each cat's nose pad is unique, just like every human's fingerprints are unique.

My nose is connected to a special scent **organ** in the roof of my mouth. It is called the Jacobson's organ. This organ helps me sniff out a possible mate, a strange cat in my territory, or an unusual odor, like a fire.

24

FUN FACT

When cats drink, we stick out our tongues and curl the edges to make a shape like a spoon. Then, we pull our tongues back quickly and flip the water down our throats.

Taste and Tongues

My sense of taste is much weaker than my sense of smell. I cannot come close to matching your sense of taste. Under the **taste buds** are sense **nerves** that send taste messages to the brain. I have less than five hundred taste buds on my tongue. You have over nine thousand taste buds on yours!

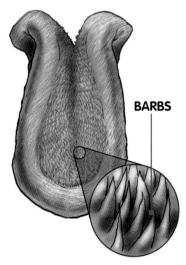

BARBS

When I lick my owners, they say my tongue feels like sand-paper. Well, it should; it's covered with lots of sharp barbs! These barbs face backward toward my throat. When I eat, these sharp barbs help scrape the meat off the bone. When I groom myself, they act like a hairbrush. As I lick my fur, my **saliva** works like soap.

Cleo's Clues

Cats are used to eating canned cat food from the fridge. When cats eat in the wild, however, their fresh kill is warm. We still like our food that way. Warm food lets off lots of odors that we really enjoy. If it is not too much trouble, please heat your cat's food or take it out of the refrigerator early so it can warm up on its own.

STAYING IN TOUCH

I have an uncle who is blind, but he can still get around his home and yard quite easily. He uses his whiskers. Whiskers help cats the same way that fingertips help humans. They let us feel our world.

A special kind of hair, whiskers are stiff, strong, and twice as thick as my other hair. A whisker's roots go three times deeper than the roots of normal hair. Many nerves and **blood vessels** surround them.

I have twelve stiff whiskers that grow in four rows on each side of my nose above my upper lip. The upper two rows of whiskers can move separately from the lower two rows.

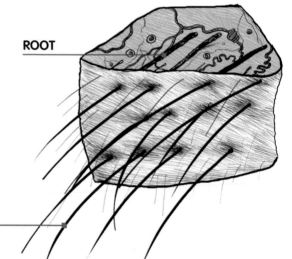

ROOT

WHISKERS

FUN FACT
We also have other small groups of whiskers above each eye and on the backs of our front paws.

Sensing Size and Shape

When whiskers move even a tiny bit, the nerves at the roots can sense the change. With a whisper of a breeze, my whiskers **vibrate**, and I can feel it. As air flows through a room and hits furniture, the air movements shift. My whiskers let me feel these shifts. They help me sense the size and shape of objects without actually seeing or touching them.

The whiskers on my face stick out as far as the widest part of my body, so I can use them to measure a small opening. If my whiskers won't fit through a hole, the rest of me won't either.

Cleo's Clue

Please do not trim your cat's whiskers. It will lessen his ability to feel his way around.

GLOSSARY

ancient — relating to a time long ago

blood vessels — small tubes in the body through which blood travels

catnip — a strong-smelling herb that attracts cats

eventually — at some unknown later time

flexible — able to bend and stretch easily

incredible — so unusual that it may seem impossible

mummies — bodies treated and prepared for burial in a way that somewhat preserves them

nerves — special cells that join together and carry signals to and from the brain

organ — a part of the body, such as the heart, lungs, stomach, or liver, that does a specific job

prey — describing animals that are eaten by other animals

saliva — the liquid made in the mouth; spit

surroundings — the area that an animal lives in

taste buds — groups of cells in the mouth or throat that form tiny bumps and are connected to nerves that send taste information to the brain

vertebra — one of a series of a bony segments that make up the spine

vet — short for *veterinarian*, a doctor who takes care of animals

vibrate — to move back and forth or side to side very quickly

worship — to treat with great respect and honor as a god or goddess

BOOKS

Everything Cat: What Kids Really Want to Know About Cats. Kids' FAQs (series). Marty Crisp (Northword Press)

How to Talk to Your Cat. Jean Craighead George (HarperTrophy)

Totally Fun Things to Do with Your Cat. Play with Your Pet (series). Maxine Rock (Jossey-Bass)

Why Do Cats Meow? Easy-to-Read (series). Joan Holub (Puffin)

WEB SITES

ASPCA Animaland Pet Care
www.aspca.org/site/PageServer?pagename = kids_pc_cat_411
Find out basic facts about cats and how to care for them. You can also click on a link to watch Pet Care Cartoons.

Cats International
www.catsinternational.org
Check out the library of articles on this educational organization's Web site dedicated to helping people better understand their cats.

Fact Monster: Pets
factmonster.info/pets.html
Scroll down to find articles on cats on this site, which has information about many kinds of pets.

Your Pet Cat
www.bbc.co.uk/cbbc/wild/pets/cat.shtml
Click on this interactive site to learn loads about your cat and its behavior.

INDEX

ABOUT THE AUTHOR

John Burstein (also known as Slim Goodbody) has been entertaining and educating children for over thirty years. His programs have been broadcast on CBS, PBS, Nickelodeon, USA, and Discovery. He has won numerous awards including the Parent's Choice Award and the President's Council's Fitness Leader Award. Currently, Mr. Burstein tours the country with his multimedia live show "Bodyology." For more information, please visit slimgoodbody.com.